SELF BELIEF AND
NO BOUNDARIES

SELF BELIEF AND NO BOUNDARIES

Corwin Morton

authorHOUSE®

AuthorHouse™
1663 Liberty Drive
Bloomington, IN 47403
www.authorhouse.com
Phone: 1 (800) 839-8640

Published by AuthorHouse 10/12/2015

ISBN: 978-1-5049-5511-9 (sc)
ISBN: 978-1-5049-5510-2 (e)

Print information available on the last page.

This book is printed on acid-free paper.

TO ALL READ THIS BOOK

Now before I get started I do not wish to offend anybody so if I do in the course of this book I sincerely apologize if I do.

This is a book written about my life experiences in hopes that I can help many others with similar experiences.

I know that mankind has made great strides both good and bad. But it seems that with every good turn towards mankind, there have been many more turn's or strides if you will, that have either been miss used or were intentionally used as new and better ways to destroy mankind.

ABOUT THE AUTHOR

I was born in the year 1962 in a small Town of falls city Nebraska. And I have lived through things that probably should never have been, I have seen things both good and bad, and I've turned many of bad situation into a good situation by thinking it through and seeing the beauty and all things. I have taken the impossible, and made it probable as well as in some cases reality. And I have taken can't and turned it into can do. I have foreseen the possibilities before is all, and used a can do attitude in everything. I have found ways to make anything possible, and I ask all of you who read this to do the same, why?

<u>Because you can,where there is a will there is a way</u> !.

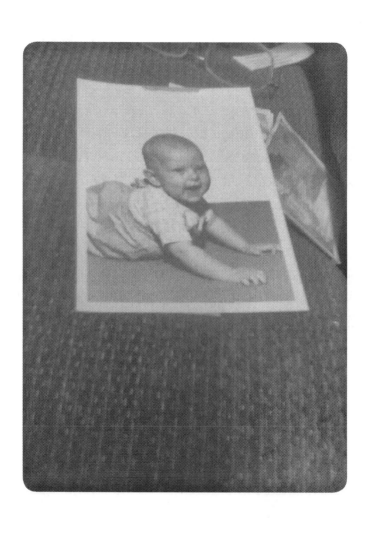

Now this is a picture of me when I was 6 months of age 4 months before my car accident, and this is me at 7 months three months before my accident

And in 1963 I had a car accident I was only 10 months of age,

Now in the picture above its 1967 I believe, and it's Christmas. I'm wearing the helmet because that time I had some very sensitive plating in my head protect and restore the missing fourth of my skull.

I've been through a lot more operations and procedures then I care to remember one of those procedures was known as at that time as an experimental ventricular peritoneal shunting system and for those of you don't know exactly what that is it's basically a tube with a valve that regulates fluids and drains excessive fluids from your brain down to your kidneys so that one can dispose of them, I also had a great many chemicals put in me, courtesy of Medical Science and their so called advancements again some of those were experimental.

So I suppose you can say I was used as a guinea pig whereas some of these things some worked some didn't. I had most of these procedures done between the ages of 10 months 21 years of age. I'm told, that a lot of these chemicals and things have not broken down in my system yet and possibly never will.

I've done things that have both been medically, scientifically, psychologically, and humanly impossible or at least improbable, and to everybody's surprise I make them work for me, so I prove everybody wrong by doing all those things and more. You see, in my early years I never succumbed to negative emotions I had a **can do** attitude you could say. And Some of those things I speak of were; trying to go to school when others said I couldn't because I could not sit still, I could not focus in on what was being said, so basically I could not learn, these were some of the excuses or false facts that I was given all to discourage me from ever trying, all because of my head trauma. And yes like every other kid I was picked on for being different as well as looking different.

However having a very strong military background family and being somewhat of an army brat myself. I had the help of the many veterans from both Korean era, and Vietnam era with the help of my father whom I believe was a staff sergeant at the time.

The United States Army and they're saying *"**be all that you can be**"* and the United States Marines and they're saying, "**the few the proud the Marines**" *"never give up!* "thus I always seem to have the support I needed when I needed it the most, we lived in many different places when I was growing up some of those places that I can recall are Panama South America for about three and a half years

This is a picture of my father bending over me one Christmas I believe that was 1967 in Panama City Panama we lived about half a block or so from the Canal Zone so we could go out on the front lawn and waved everybody coming though the Panama locks which was very exciting because some of the ships that I saw where the Queen Mary on her maiden voyage, the Queen Mary 2 on her maiden voyage, and of course I had a whole menagerie of different animals such as a dog who later had puppies, many different types of fish, both fresh water, and exotic animals such as an orangutang, a Capuchin monkey, and somehow a rattler snake that scared my mother had gotten in the apartment complex was hiding behind refrigerator because it was cool, and when my mother open the refrigerator door; well you get the picture, I also had several parakeets and other birds, a gecko lizard and a few other things I can't remember to well. And what I could not learn in school I learned from these animals as well as the folklore and legends of the country, of course many genre of science fiction taught me to think because they never had any problems with their society and if they did they help them out instead of shut them out thus some of my favorite authors gene Roddenberry, Isaac Asimov, Yolanda McIntire, to name a few these all inspired me to keep going.

So the people who are reading this, and some people before you, probably did everything you could to keep me going through the sixty's up to now. So now it is my turn: **to read this and let it sink in** and thus you can find something to call your own finding out that you are important! for me, yourself, and everyone around you regardless, so you must keep going.

My name is Corwin Howard Morton the third MD and this is my story; some of which I've already told you but I shall continue with a little bit more,

I hold a great many doctorates, titles about somewhere in the neighborhood of a about 45 maybe 50 different areas, and a couple of bachelors degrees in computers and in law, and an associate's degree in police sciences and humanity.

And at the time of me writing this book I am 53 years of age and I have accomplished great deeds, **notice the picture above me,** that's was taken at Fort Snelling Cemetery during Memorial Day of 2015, that was of me and the director of the Veterans Hospital here in Bloomington Minnesota.

However, as I'm told by many veterans and civilians that I've helped in the hospitals and so on and so forth I have helped through life or inspiration. That I've been through hell and back mainly because I've done so much and been through so much In this lifetime.

You see for some time now I've been a Ward missionary of the Church of Jesus Christ of Latter day Saints, I've also been for the past 40 years or so a chaplain for the Sons of the American Legion not the mention, some have called me the miracle son or boy and helper of mankind, so I guess I can call myself a veteran of sorts.

Now if I go back in time - 1962 May 18th which was the day of my birth, my mother and father were both proud to have a son I was their first born. And to my knowledge I was supposed to have a sister with me unfortunately she was stillborn the car accident it took a fourth of my skull and left me possibly brain-damage with a possible 15% chance to live of course this was 10 month later in 1963. My mother was told I had a touch of epilepsy and because of my car accident that led to severe blood loss, and loss of my 4th of the skull,I would most likely never amount anything except maybe a couch potato for life that's if I lived I was given a chance possibly 24 to 36 hours to live however if I did live I could never sit still in school or anything else for that matter, and I could never possibly learn anything.

Thus I went through my early years questioning everything and doing some things in my own way, instead of trying to do what everybody else told me, I could never do or was impossible for me. And this might sound funny to you however with the help of such things as Twilight Zone, outer limits, lost in space, the prisoner, and one of my other favorites Star Trek I began to self teach myself to do things other people called impossible, 4 things you'll never do or can't do.

I took on the idea, that as your mom always told you when you were growing up" can't never did anything, and nothing is impossible!" and did you know if you believe in yourself you can accomplish anything if you want to do it! so what she said is true. And with the United States Army, drilling into my head the 21 years of my life in the hospital out of the hospitals "suck it up," be all you can be and never give up!" you are our mascot and inspiration to keep going so you have to live up to our motto for us as much as For you. Infact that's also what I liked about Gene Roddenberry's vision Star Trek to quote him" anything is possible, all you have to do is keep reaching for the stars and if you believe you can do anything'.

So as I said earlier I got off my butt and started self-teaching myself, and asking questions I went to school regardless of what people said i did this in my own way and I did my best to mimic what other students did so that I could sit still in class and learn as they did, of course i repeated because we moved around a lot. And that was both good and bad good in the means that I got to learn alot of things and languages that I didn't get to learn in school.

However Star Trek was always there for me, that was one show that I took the heart because yes everybody was different but we all got along regardless. And nobody said no! about anything, that was one of the things I liked about it, and aside from the military veterans and soldiers kept me going Star Trek kept me questioning things like "Who am I?" "why am I here?" "why can I not do what other kids can do?". And why do people keep saying No! you can't do this or that, or that's impossible for you, this presented a challenge for me.

And so between my medical appointments and my psychological appointments I begin doing things that everybody else told me I couldn't do self teaching myself and eventually going to school, many schools and in between this I was told I was hoping now people in my situation and Beyond. thought I was adopted so to speak as a military mascot of sorts some called me a miracle boy, a veteran of sorts, because I kept pushing the limit aka doing things that were medically physically and psychologically impossible but for me they were possible because I made them that way. Ironically in amusing sorta way I made these doctors rewrite books of the status quo for human beings as to what's impossible and what's probable.

As I was growing up I played games with and paled around with favorite musicians and actors such as Nat King Cole an up-and-coming country western singer, Elvis Presley the king of rock and roll, Leonard Nimoy (Spock on Star Trek), DeForest Kelley (Doctor Leonard bones McCoy on Star Trek) to name a few. And I was in the news several times from my hospital rooms wherever they might be at the time. Throughout my lifetime I also was on many Kiddie shows when I was younger, the ones I can remember were in Panama South America as well as in later years a couple times in St Paul Minneapolis and in Bemidji Minnesota (I think it was) Camp Courage with the name of the place and we had visits from roundhouse Rodney, and Casey Jones, Jerry Lewis sometimes and Captain Kangaroo.

It was there that i learned how to horseback ride.

Thus, my belief that anything is possible, can't never did anything! And if you can help it never give up. And I hope as you read this, It inspires you as well to listen to everybody and to try and decide for yourself or have somebody help you, because! *You are important, the LORD thy God made us all and he wouldn't have taken time to make us and give us the choice to come here on earth if we didn't deserve a chance thus we must make her own destiny if we must have help then so be it but do not let others make it for you your destiny that is,* you see as I have said and as I have implied: you can do anything you put your mind to that's if you want to do it.! And this statement I shall make several times through this book as you are the reader I need you to take this to heart.

Now during my time in between school when I wasn't helping somebody deal with life situations, I was volunteering for trying to tutor other kids in school, or working things like: MDA Muscular Dystrophy Association, CEDA Citizen Education Development Association, programs or I took a Correspondence course or two in learning police sciences, private investigation, building inspection / housing inspection. Of course then I also went through Junior High and high school I got good grades because of course I had to study harder then the kids and of course I have a lot more questions about things maybe not the right things but things. I learned to drive a car in the eighty's however after several attempts of passing the drivers test,written test, road test, I kept making a mistake of telling my mother so after mutual consent between us she won I chose not to drive.

Instead I learn the bus system many times over does the Metro bus system kept changing I also acquired Metro mobility to help me out and from time to time I got help from friends either at church church church or at Church

Church or acquaintances at the American Legion Post/ Squadron 1 I also chose to try and learn how to ride a 2 wheeled bicycle yes of course my mother was also against because of my obvious head trauma, however, my aunt who is taking care of me while my mother worked decided one afternoon supervise me and teach me how to ride a bike this went on for about almost 2 weeks before my mother found out and I was quite good at riding a bike at least by that time. its funny I never seemed to recognize fully that I had a disability I just had a little more to learn than others and sometimes I wanted people to notice I had a disability, and other times I wanted them not to notice. While is true that I was not exactly the easiest to get along with, I did have a way of figuring out things that others didn't and I didn't feel the need for excuses on not to do things. Through the years I had a variety of jobs one such job was the Triple A furnace cleaning service another one was Olympic Decathlon Club, as well as the St Louis Park schools system janitorial program. when I left St Louis Park for downtown Minneapolis I picked up a job working security with the St.paul Minneapolis International Airport working Central Security Services as a post baggage screener eventually I worked my way up to a supervisor position in charge of all security checkpoints in the airport, at that same time I had worked myself up to being trusted by the airlines to work as a glorified babysitter for underaged minors traveling alone aka(UMS) and foreign speaking people aka(FSPs) you didn't seem to understand they had missed their flight connection and had to stay over for 12 or 24 hours for the next one. during that time I had chance to study up on forensics for the police department as well as my criminal law studies. I worked for about five or six different companies that did security out of the

airport and during that time unfortunately I got involved in a hit-and-run accident which took my legs the knees down and put me in a coma for 6 months as well as re- splitting my head open and doing some rather nasty things to the rest of my body, again as in multiple times before I was told I'd never be able to walk again I laughed at this and said Dr. you don't know me very well do you? and with my body cast on I walked across the room to my mother's arms I might have fallen a couple times but I was determined, a couple weeks later when I got my body cast off I went downstairs and exercise on the stationary bike and while I was down there I worked on my upper arm strength did some setups and pushups did whatever I could limber my legs back up so I could walk as I said before I refused to give up. And as you probably surmised I am walking yes I need a reinforced leg brace still and yes now that I'm older I need a walking staf to help me get around but still I surprise myself let her let alone surprise you by my ability to do what everybody else claims they can't do by excuse. I volunteer my time to help those in need such as our United States veterans, various soup kitchens, homeless shelters, security firms, and the list goes on and on and on...

One would think that be the end my story I of course it is not, at this time I was living at 2432 1st Avenue South and had been working so much that I very rarely got sleep and somebody requested my help at an address several blocks away so I went to their aid to help them out and they ask for a personal blessing which I gave them for the sick it was about 8:30 at night on November 13th which of course is my mother's birthday. I figured I'd give the blessings of this person and go home call mom wish her a happy birthday however that was not to be the case as you read earlier. It was not my intention to give her a

birthday present of me in the hospital because of this hit and run accident. However again <u>did I give up</u>! **No**! <u>In the matter of speaking</u> I got up and I moved on, why is that? I think deep down inside myself it's because God has a plan for me. I told this story only a few times I know it to be true but others think that I made it up; I was asked what I remember of that night I said it was scary at first because it was dark out that after all this happened I remember a vision of an angel coming down from the heavens she reached out to me with one hand, and simply said **get up car when it's not your time! she help me across the street and I went home two or three blocks home I saw my roommate and I told him not to bother me I have a headache and I went to bed in a very very dark room at which I close the door.** Now that's what I remember

However, through all this I have not given up nor shall I ever give up, with all the help that I need to give yes I have pain but when somebody needs my help I have no pain. This is the attitude that we all should have, after all; our Lord did after all to help you out anyway we can. Why is this? I make it my policy, to put everybody first before me and when they're taken care of and it's time for me to sit back and take care of myself. Now I'm not saying that this has to be everybody's policy, it just happens to be mine I try to live by our Lord Jesus Christ words and actions while at the same time believing in is father and in the Holy Ghost.

I've lived in public housing for about 30 years, 10 of those years I've been with the Minneapolis highrise resident Council executive committee. And in February 14 of the year 2000 I got married and I was happy, alas the marriage didn't last very long only about a little over 9 years because my wife died of many complications on May 21st 2009.

However in 2012 the Southside missionaries of The Church of Jesus Christ of Latter day Saints gave me a task to help I lost mother of one child to find the Lord once again this woman was from Puerto Rico and her husband had died several years before however when he was alive he forbade anyone in his household to ever go to church or to read scripture in the household, so I got in touch person. And read scripture to her every night and if she had a question about them I would explain it, I did this for a number of years and eventually on August 11th 2014 i baptize this woman, and confirmed her in the name of Jesus Christ of Latter day Saints,

And on September 9 2015 I received a two year appointment from the mayor of Minneapolis to the disability Council for the city of Minneapolis Minnesota. This was very exciting to me, and another milestone for me to conquer so I'm going to be trying for another City Hall appointment and I'm hoping to get this: it's for high-rise resident Minneapolis Public Housing authority Council / commissioner program which is another 2 year appointment to be made by the mayor of Minneapolis.

And still I don't give up!, so if I know I said some things in here several times over. but they need to be said and you need the hear of them if I never gave up and I never will, I want you to reach for the stars please! and never give up remember, where there is a will there is a way.

So what can I say life goes on and we must go on with it, and remember;

Can't never did anything, and nothing is impossible, if you want to do it and you have the strength and willpower to do it then go for it! don't wait for others to tell you you can't or that's impossible because they know nothing.

The Lord has given us many things and we must trust in him, as we trust in our self's and as; President Kennedy said: ask not, what your country can do, but what you can do for your country and I will add for yourself.!

And may God bless america! this is land of the free, and the home of the brave. I salute you!.

So what can I tell you! Life goes on and we must move with it I'm in the second chapter of my life and it's not over yet. don't let it be over for you.

Life is but a book, and each book has chapters, this is one of my many chapters. My life work has not ended neither shall

yours. help somebody out in your own way to be an inspiration to them As I am trying to do for many.

God bless you may you find your path as I found mine with the help of others, thus you can help them find their path. So yes I have bad legs, and yes I have a messed up lumbar region of my back, and yes I have messed up knee caps, along with the messed up left side of my body and a fourth of my skull missing and live in 24/7 pain migraines and all.

<u>But as God is my witness I will never give up!</u>

Do all my problems make me disabled?

My answer is No!

Yes my body is messed up, and yes I have all these problems the deal with, however as I said before if somebody needs my help I am there. Despite my problems

So to all those who read this book, I ask you all not to give up the fight, remember if you believe you can accomplish anything God is on your side. and if you do I salute you.

Printed in the United States
By Bookmasters